Poems For
The One I Love

ALSO BY BRUCE B. WILMER

High On A Limerick

Feelings

Love Poems

Believe In Yourself
Poems of Purpose

Time Cries
A Poet's Response to 9/11/01

Poems To Carry With You
On Life's Journey:
Inspiration and Encouragement
For Every New Beginning

Poems For
The One I Love

by Bruce B. Wilmer

Published by:

Winding Brook Press
P. O. Box 7, Burnsville, NC 28714

This book is a compilation of new poems
and poems previously copyrighted by the author
in his books of poetry, FEELINGS and LOVE POEMS,
and his Light Lines® Originals poetry products

Cover photo and design by Bruce B. Wilmer

Interior photo by Jeremy B. Wilmer

http://www.brucebwilmer.com

Printed in the United States of America

ISBN: 978-1-57158-004-7

For Sydney,
who gave my heart
a place to grow

INTRODUCTION

Poems For The One I Love is an affirmation of my love affair with the girl I married forty-four years ago. It is a book about love, not marriage. It started with my first love poem, "The Perfect Two," written in 1976, seven years after our marriage. It tracks our life together with affection and surprise and looks to the future with optimism and hope. The book expands and updates my 1990 book, *Love Poems*, and gives further substance to my proclamation at that time that love need never grow old. Its new beginnings and rediscoveries give youth a constant perspective. Most importantly, it can be perfect when we're not. Like a rainbow, it stirs our sense of beauty and imagination. Nurtured and cared for, it has the resilience of stone. As with the deepest friendship, it's our anchor to the universe, our place in time, our proof that we exist, our reason for existence.

This book is not a dissertation on love, just one person's grateful testimony and statement of wonder. It plots the tender moments of time when love infused my spirit with warmth and compelled me to record my feelings. As such, it is the pulse of my love, read over time. It is a tribute to the carefree, innocent and caring moments that have liberated my heart and pen. Foremost, it is a portrait of my wife, Sydney, whose loving acceptance over the years and beautiful spirit gave my heart a place to grow.

—Bruce B. Wilmer
Western NC (2013)

CONTENTS

Before I met you I was just
   A lonely dream in flight,
A heart without an anchor,
   A season without light.

from Before I Met You (page 201)

Poems For
The One I Love

New Love

I'M GLAD I MET YOU

Our paths converged and softly touched—
    Our hearts moved close in greeting.
It was a time to sample change—
    It was a time for meeting.

An accident of chance became
    Our lasting gift that day.
Some paths may cross but do not always
    Join in such a way.

I'm glad you've shared your life with me
    And made this moment prime.
The future will preserve the warmth
    That fills this precious time.

The present is a prize
    That you have helped to make complete.
I'm glad that fate arranged a way
    For you and me to meet.

OUR LIVES TOUCHED

Love had but a little while,
  So love made me your friend.
The time thus spared, so briefly shared,
  Was all love had to lend.

I loved you for that moment
  When lives did briefly touch.
But in its way love wouldn't say
  How lasting or how much.

If life gives us another chance,
  We'll have the time to see
If love will have the patience
  To favor you and me.

But since we cannot hope to know
  Just what the future sends,
Let's value what we found together
  Knowing we were friends.

BUT FOR CHANCE

But for chance, some paths don't cross,
   Some moments don't occur.
But for crystals formed in time,
   Some images just blur.

But for little accidents
   That turn our lives and change them,
Major forces wouldn't find
   Our dreams and rearrange them.

But for certain key events
   That interrupt our stride,
Worldly possibilities
   Would never seem so wide.

Losses, even setbacks,
   May propel our lives ahead.
Negatives may motivate
   And launch our goals instead.

Love may flourish, hopes may grow,
   And friendships may advance
Because of that imposing little
   Factor known as chance.

FIRST MEETING

I saw you across the room,
   Singled out of the group's lively conversing
As a solitary flower, sharply defined.

The blur of all else swirled around
   My heightened awareness of you,
Driving my evening toward the single objective
   Of meeting you amidst the confusion
     Of this chance encounter.

Words, now unremembered, consummated this
   Cosmic convergence of two lives,
This improbable crossing of paths
   Which drew our hearts from random orbit
     Into common trajectory.

What distant launch of spirit
   Could have programmed this moment
     So accurately.
What sudden transfusion of heart
   Implanted the moment forever
     In our shared consciousness.

This touch of time
　　Could have been a near miss.
Our souls might have then roamed
　　The vastness forever,
　　　　Thwarted by fate,
Unaware that heaven had opened a crack
　　And for one brief moment
　　　　Let our mortal eyes
　　　　　　View the possibility
　　　　　　　　Of each other.

WE HAD FUN TOGETHER

We had a lot of fun together,
  Got along so well,
That in my mind a host of rather
  Pleasant thoughts still dwell.

All the time we shared rushed by;
  Too soon our day had ended.
It's satisfying when two paths
  Have crossed and lives have blended.

There's so much more for us to learn,
  New thoughts we can exchange,
New feelings we can introduce,
  More sharing to arrange.

I hope you felt the same as I,
  Enjoyed the time completely.
It's hard for me to comprehend
  What all this means concretely.

But I just couldn't let
  This special moment disappear
Without informing you how much
  It meant to have you near.

I ENJOY BEING WITH YOU

I enjoy the time when I'm with you;
  I'm happy when we're talking.
I value all the things we do,
  The quiet moments walking.

So many things are better shared;
  And I'm so glad that we
Find such complete fulfillment in
  Each other's company.

There's more to life when you're around;
  You make me feel alive.
There's nothing I withhold from you;
  With you, my passions thrive.

I'm able to explore my thoughts,
  Relax in freedom found.
The confidence I feel is
  Reassuring and profound.

The moments we're together
  Are such special ones for me,
Because I sense that we exist
  In loving harmony.

IF IT ONLY LASTS FOR NOW

If it only lasts for now,
  It's something special still.
If it is this moment's gift
  To cherish, then I will.

If it's but a fleeting flame
  We find in our today,
I know its tender message
  Will remain, not drift away.

If it is tomorrow's choice
  To say, let's now move on,
The memories within our hearts
  Won't fade and then be gone.

If it's only for today,
  This precious time let's claim;
For this is one pure moment
  When our hearts feel much the same.

YOU'RE SPECIAL TO ME

You're special to me—
    You're someone I trust.
I treasure the topics
    That we have discussed.

I'm thankful for times
    You have summoned a smile.
I'm grateful our paths
    Have converged for a while.

I'm pleased by each confidence
    You have displayed.
I cherish those moments
    You've sought to persuade.

I'm touched by the gestures
    Of kindness you've shown.
I've noticed how fast
    All our hours have flown.

I'm feeling the force
    Of a friendship that's true.
I'm fortunate knowing
    A person like you.

I CARE FOR YOU

The moods of my mind
    Softly whisper and weave,
And the message I'm hearing
    Refuses to leave...
                I care for you.

In a world that is changing,
    As old patterns shift,
There's a recurrent meaning,
    A general drift...
                I care for you.

No incidents past
    Or memories now
Can silence the feelings
    That my thoughts allow...
                I care for you.

Relationships change
    And people do, too;
But a constant emotion
    Keeps filtering through...
                I care for you.

FINDING LOVE AGAIN

After life has lost its love
     And *now* erases *then,*
The lonely heart may choose the path
     Of finding love again.

The past will never fade and go
     Entirely away.
The beauty and the tragedy
     Are in the soul to stay.

But all that lives in memory
     Gives hope a new dimension.
A loss endured should not place love
     Forever in suspension.

The seasoned heart needs once again
     To feel a life of caring.
Two solitary lives can be
     Enriched through times of sharing.

Two hearts that look again for love
     Will find their passion strong.
Two lives that link in harmony
     Will sing a better song.

TWO FREE

My independence gives me freedom
    Only to be free;
But freedom tells me there is something
    I alone can't be.

For freedom's very private voice
    Must have a private hearing;
And selfless listening can't be found
    Without two people sharing.

Freedom's body, too, must find
    Through warmth its definition.
Alone its fires turn to cold
    Just wanting recognition.

And freedom's soul must find a match;
    New strength it must inherit.
If freedom grows, it's when it knows
    It's found a kindred spirit.

I'LL WAIT FOR YOU

I know that you're not ready yet—
    Your love I won't pursue;
But while you're making up your mind,
    My love will wait for you.

A love that's freely chosen
    Is a love that will endure.
A love that is prepared to wait
    Will end up more secure.

My love for you is something
    That I never will outgrow.
I'll wait until you're sure enough
    To answer yes or no.

And if you should decide that love
    Is not for us to share,
I hope that you will tell me so
    And your true thoughts declare.

But if you sense that love describes
    The feeling in your heart,
Then share with me your deepest thoughts
    So we're not long apart.

YOU'RE MORE THAN A FRIEND

I have a special feeling
    That I scarcely comprehend.
In my deepest thoughts I sense
    You're more than just a friend.

I wouldn't want to rush us now
    As friendship we explore;
But there's a growing warmth inside
    That I just can't ignore.

I enjoy our times together—
    We're so comfortable and free.
I think of you when I'm alone—
    I think of you and me.

I feel that we have much to share,
    Warm secrets to uncover.
There is a whole lot more to life
    That we can both discover.

I don't know where we're heading
    Or just where this road will end.
But you're truly someone special
    Who is more than just a friend.

TOGETHER

If life is full of challenge
  And gives us outstretched wings,
Let's soar to highest places
  And discover many things...
                together.

If life reveals its message
  To open eyes and ears,
Let's savor all the beauty
  And conquer any tears...
                together.

If life is meant for sharing
  And time forever runs,
Let's find our hidden moments
  And chase the setting sun...
                together.

If life is meant for loving
  And love is meant for two,
Let's never waste a moment
  Nor ever miss a cue...
                together.

If life is ever lonely
  And two are ever free,
Let us recall the moments
  When life placed you and me...
                together.

YOU'RE SO MUCH MORE

When I think of others
    I have met and known before,
Nothing in my thoughts compares with you—
    You're so much more.

I can't ignore the feelings
    That are rushing through my heart—
I feel we've been together
    Longer than we've been apart.

Our spirits seem to know each other;
    Thoughts exist in phase.
Life is pure sensation
    Softly shared a thousand ways.

A knowledge and a comfort
    Fills my feelings to the core.
I know that I am one with you,
    Because you're so much more.

SHARE WITH ME

Share with me your inner world;
 Reveal to me your thinking.
Tell me when your spirits soar,
 Or even when they're sinking.

Share with me your every mood.
 Permit me to explore
Your hopes and aspirations—
 Let me know you to the core.

Share with me your true concerns,
 Perplexities and fears.
Share your strengths and weaknesses...
 And don't conceal your tears.

Share with me your fantasies,
 Your loves and your obsessions.
Let me understand your wants
 And savor your impressions.

Let me know your inner warmth
 And share your inner flame.
Tell me all there is to know,
 And I will do the same.

SINCE WE MET

Since we met, I'm more alive—
    I see the days more clearly.
There's a glowing in my heart—
    I weigh the hours dearly.

Since we fully gave ourselves
    And touched in ways of caring,
We opened up the infinite,
    Unleashed the light of sharing.

You satisfy the hunger
    That inhabits hearts alone
And fill me with the passion
    That your tenderness has sown.

We fill a special space in time,
    A universe of two.
I share the world of now
    In heart and mind with only you.

NEW LOVE

Our love is young and has
    The fragile beauty of a rose;
But whether life will let
    Its form endure, time only knows.

If we allow these moments
    To inspire feelings new,
We'll gaze upon tomorrow
    As a time for me and you.

But if we fail to nourish
    The emotions love has built,
Then all its vital freshness
    Will too soon begin to wilt.

In this sweet moment I can't guess
    If love will choose to stay.
But I'm content to cherish
    Its rare form from day to day.

THROUGH OUR EYES

Through my eyes, look into me—
    See things no one has seen.
Gaze a while, see a smile,
    Let nothing come between.
Discover all and then some more;
    Find facets never found.
Let my eyes tell everything
    Without a single sound.

Through your eyes will I perceive
    The infinite in you—
The crystal maze that time surveys
    And life brings into view.
I'll gather in your brightest rays,
    Discover hidden talents;
I'll penetrate the mystery
    Of lives and hearts in balance.

I'll look at you and you at me—
    Our eyes will talk together.
Our meanings will traverse the air
    As softly as a feather.
We'll know the truth that words and deeds
    Don't have the time to tell;
And through our eyes shall I in you
    And you in me e'er dwell.

COME SHARE MY LIFE

I've wandered through the forest
    And heard its sounds alone.
I've seen a robin hopping
    And paused where moss has grown.

I've thrown a pebble seaward
    While walking on the sand.
I've sat and watched the waves break
    And gathered shells in hand.

I've seen the autumn colors
    And hiked through winter snow.
I've felt the summer rainfall
    And watched spring flowers grow.

I've savored life in moments past,
    But now I understand—
There's more to life if we can share it
    Walking hand in hand.

SEARCHING ENDED

What in the mix
    Of spirits blended
Tells the tale
    Of searching ended.

What in the truth
    Of minds believing
Talks of isolation
    Leaving.

What in the press
    Of two hearts beating
Sounds a story
    Worth repeating.

What in the warmth
    Of two lives clasping
Makes tomorrow
    So worth grasping.

What in the touch
    Of each day's sun
Takes our two paths
    And makes them one.

Intense Love

I NEED YOU

It seems you're always in my dreams—
    You fill my waking hours.
Your presence and your promise
    Warm me with their magic powers.

My heart's in disarray—My mind
    Is reeling with distraction.
My body feels for yours
    An irresistible attraction.

Whenever we're apart, that sense
    Of emptiness starts growing.
But when you're close to me,
    My world is filled to overflowing.

My thoughts all lead to passion—
    My emotions fully heed you.
Each moment, every bit of me
    Keeps saying that I need you.

LISTEN TO MY HEART

Come close to me and let me show you
    Where my feelings start.
Come close to where affections flow
    And listen to my heart.

Remove the distance in between
    That makes us feel as two.
Let us press our hearts together,
    Vital links renew.

Magnify the force of love
    That bonds our life as one.
Let our chemistry together
    Be our inner sun.

Hear the pounding message
    Of two bodies taking part,
And let the word of love be spoken
    Softly to the heart.

YOU ARE MY INSPIRATION

You are my inspiration,
  My source of energy.
You stimulate my senses;
  You set my spirits free.

You liberate my thinking;
  You captivate my heart.
You redefine my vision;
  You magnify my art.

You stir my independence;
  You sentence me for life
To see your sweeter meanings—
  You still the outer strife.

You bring me close to nature;
  You share with me its truth.
You rush me into springtime;
  You exercise my youth.

You make all time seem precious—
  Life's essence you enhance.
You fill my days with wonder
  And exquisite romance.

A CORNER OF MY HEART

A corner of my heart
   Will always be reserved for you.
A corner of my consciousness
   Lets all your light shine through.

A corner of my senses
   Cannot shed your touch and feel.
A corner of my world
   Is very fresh and very real.

A corner of my daily hopes and dreams
   Has you in mind.
A corner of each breathing moment
   Wants our breath combined.

A corner of my spirit
   Finds in you a place that's free.
Your corner of my life
   Is now a major part of me.

SOMETHING HAPPENED IN MY HEART

Something happened in my heart
    A breath or two ago.
Its rhythm skipped and raced a bit
    And caused an inner glow.

I lost a breath as I drew in
    A fleeting thought of you.
I held the thought inside me—
    Then I let it filter through.

The warmth that it awakened,
    The feelings that it stirred
Gently notified me
    Something special had occurred.

For as I drew into my heart
    Your image passing through,
I knew that I had lost a breath
    And skipped a beat for you.

A SECRET FEELING

A secret emotion,
 A most private feeling
Is stirring affections
 That I've been concealing.

My heart doesn't know
 Why these feelings have started.
My thoughts rush to sensuous
 Regions uncharted.

My dreams are not rational,
 Based on clear thinking.
My logic and reason
 Are rapidly shrinking.

I'm not in control
 Of my inner emotions.
I'm lost in a pack
 Of impossible notions.

My senses are drowning
 In passionate scenes.
I cannot quite fathom
 What all of this means.

You've entered my thinking—
 I'm no more the same.
I'm feeling distracted—
 You're clearly to blame!

OUR SECRET LOVE

In inner space our lives embrace;
    In softness I discover
How you in sheltered moments
    Have become my friend, my lover.

In secret places love erases
    The innocence of friends.
In warming ways we touch in praise
    And closeness never ends.

In vision's eye our looks supply
    A feast of forms to know.
In sensual disclosure
    We have nothing left to show.

With intimate intentions,
    Through mutual desires,
For friendliest of reasons,
    My heart with yours conspires.

YOU'RE A PART OF ME

I share the flow of life with you;
  I feel the things you feel;
I sense your moments of concern,
  The depths that you reveal.

My spirit filters into you,
  As yours slips into mine.
I think of us as just one person
  As our hearts combine.

I draw you close and gather in
  Your gifts of energy.
Our one-and-one are meshed as two,
  And two blend perfectly.

We're closer than we've ever been—
  We're unified in dreams.
There's joy in our together—
  We are living precious themes.

Eternity has lent us space—
  Our moments are too few.
I'm grateful that you're part of me,
  And I am part of you.

Love Across The Miles

YOU ARE ON MY MIND

Something in my inner space
    Would like to bridge the miles.
Something in the way I miss you
    Seems the worst of trials.

Something in the feelings
    That are kindled in my heart
Stirs the warmth and then the cold
    Of knowing we're apart.

Something in my memory
    That teases me so much
Is trying to recapture
    The true essence of your touch.

Something in the fleeting thoughts
    That merge both joy and pain
Makes the passions of the heart
    Much harder to contain.

Something in my quiet moments
    Seems at once so dear
When thoughts of you can crystallize
    Into a joyful tear.

Something in the way the heart
    A ray of warmth can find
Reminds me of just how I feel
    When you are on my mind.

I WILL MISS YOU

You are the bright ingredient
    In every passing day
That life and change and circumstance
    Now softly steal away.

You're moving to the future,
    Hitching to a distant star.
The goals that you are following
    Are taking you afar.

My heart will travel with you,
    And my hopes will bless your course.
My world of joy reluctantly
    Bids farewell to its source.

That's not to say that thoughts of you
    Won't lighten every day.
But now I look with longing
    For that extra special ray.

Your presence is a luxury
    My memory enshrines.
The sun is not as vivid
    When your image elsewhere shines.

But for each empty feeling
    That my lonely heart must learn
There is the corresponding joy
    That comes when you return.

YOU'RE JUST A THOUGHT AWAY

Distance takes us far apart
    And darkens my today.
I have to keep remembering—
    You're just a thought away.

When the world is too confusing,
    Times are hard to bear,
I pull your precious meaning,
    Your bright spirit, from the air.

If I sometimes drift into
    A lonely state of mind,
I gather up the memories
    Of days we left behind.

And though you're not beside me,
    I can tap into my heart
And draw upon the warmth and love
    That lives when we're apart.

And with these fond reflections
    On the times when you were near,
I sense a little bit of what
    It's like to have you here.

WHEN WE ARE APART

In matters of the heart
    I have a weakness that is clear—
I can't imagine loneliness
    As long as you are near.

But when I can't be with you
    And I'm feeling all alone,
The sense of isolation
    Is the greatest I have known.

While we are close together,
    I am blissfully aware
That I am truly happy
    Merely knowing you are there.

But when we are apart,
    The very opposite is true—
I am totally distracted
    Merely knowing there is you.

I MISS YOU

A little bit of you
    And a little bit of me
Have switched respective places
    In a mystifying "we."

When miles come between us
    And our lives are drawn apart,
Our thoughts remain together
    Tugging softly at the heart.

This loneliness without you
    Tells of special moments shared
And says across the miles
    Just how much we've always cared.

The emptiness that comes
    With just the memory of your touch
Stirs a feeling from within that says,
    "I miss you very much."

YOU FILL MY THOUGHTS

In tender ways
    I often find
You fill my thoughts—
    You're on my mind.

In cherished moments
    I can sense
You give my thoughts
    Their eloquence.

In fond reflections
    Through the day
I think of you
    In every way.

In fleeting glimpses
    Of the past
The thoughts of you
    Are those that last.

In times apart
    I've always known
Through thoughts of you
    I'm not alone.

I'M THINKING OF YOU

My mind is moving silently,
    Fond memories selecting.
I linger long with thoughts of you,
    Remembering, reflecting.

In moments when the mind is free
    It makes impromptu choices;
And as it drifts from thought to thought
    It summons certain voices.

When time permits my thoughts to drift
    Through tides of fond recall,
I recreate the times we've shared,
    Those moments large and small.

And when I'm roused from reverie,
    An inner feeling yearns
For many more such moments
    When the thought of you returns.

LOVE

Love is a distance
    That wants to be less,
A joining together,
    A dream to express,

A treasure in time
    Kindly opened by chance,
Eternity's own
    Invitation to dance,

A blending of words
    That is warm to the touch,
A touch of the spirit
    Fulfilling so much,

A visit in person
    That just wants to stay,
A tender "I miss you"
    When so far away,

A hope in the heart
    Meant to grow and mature,
A song in the soul
    With a melody pure,

A fondness for time,
    Whether glacial or racing,
A passion for "us,"
    Every moment embracing.

Love is a harvest
    That lasts for all seasons,
Receiving and giving
    For warm, wondrous reasons.

Love is a mutual
    Concept of space
That beckons two people
    To share the same place.

A DAY WITHOUT YOU

It's hard to imagine
    A sky without blue,
A spring without flowers,
    A day without you.

You're so much a part
    Of my landscape of living
That I take for granted
    The treasures you're giving.

But if I attempt
    To absorb all your light
And see how your colors
    Illumine the night,

I realize that all
    That my heart reads as true
Is lost if the day
    Is a day without you.

Images Of Love

YOU ARE MY POETRY

An image growing stronger,
    A metaphor increasing,
My source of inspiration,
    You are my love unceasing.

A mood I want to capture,
    A feeling to explore,
A message from inside me,
    A thought I can't ignore.

A need to know you further,
    To let my heart expound,
A hunger to describe the inner
    Beauty I have found.

You are my heart's creation;
    You set my verses free;
You are the words I'm looking for;
    You are my poetry.

HONEYSUCKLE

Honeysuckle satisfaction,
  Honeysuckle savor.
Honeysuckle sense of sweetness,
  Filling me with flavor.

Honeysuckle perfume,
  Unannounced in your seduction,
Floating in so freely,
  Never needing introduction.

Never could I love another
  As I now love you.
No nectar to my lips
  Could match your purity so true.

And once I've sipped your faint aroma
  To intoxication,
No flower less than yours
  Will stir my fond anticipation.

DEWDROP

Life is like a flower;
    Hope is like a tear;
Love is like a dewdrop
    Awaiting to appear.

Morning is the sunlight,
    The mist a passing haze,
The dew a fragile meeting,
    A meshing with the days.

Night defines the daylight;
    It changes dew to tear;
It closes up the flower;
    It opens hope to fear.

But while the flower's open
    And dew adorns its petals,
Let's celebrate the flower
    Until the teardrop settles.

SPRING VISIT

You came to me
  On perfumed day
When spring awoke
  In early May.

You came to me
  In budding birth,
In clusters closely
  Hugging earth.

You came to me
  In whispered breeze,
In luscious wind
  And waving trees.

You came to me
  In trilling song,
In sounds to which
  The days belong.

You came to me
  In hopeful rain
And warmed the heart
  And eased the pain.

YOU'RE MY FANTASY

You are my favored fantasy,
    My island of discovery.
You elevate my spirits—
    You're my reason for recovery.

You stir my fond imaginings,
    Give reverie its fuel.
You brighten every moment—
    You're my ever precious jewel.

You stimulate my senses;
    You're the center of my thinking.
You give me hope and optimism,
    Keep my faith from shrinking.

You tutor me in passion,
    Give substance to my dreams.
You fill up my emotions,
    Let me love you to extremes.

You and I are lovers
    In that land within the heart.
Let's hope it's ours forever;
    Let's hope we'll never part.

LOVE IS A RAINBOW

Love is a rainbow
    Where true colors blend.
You are the treasure
    I find at the end.

Love is our spectrum
    Of thoughts and emotions,
Our feelings of warmth
    And affectionate notions.

Love's our invisible
    Visible force—
Our ultimate, infinite,
    Exquisite source.

Love is our fantasy
    Glimmering bright,
Life's beautiful image
    Reflecting the light.

Love is our dream
    That wants to come true—
I'm glad to be sharing
    This rainbow with you.

MY LOVE FOR YOU

My love for you
    Is like the sky,
With dreams that soar
    And hopes that fly.

It's like a
    Never ending ocean,
An everlasting,
    Deep emotion.

It has the tenderness
    Of spring,
The charm that warmth
    And laughter bring.

It has the simple
    Strength of stone.
It shields us from
    A life alone.

It's ever growing,
    Ever new.
It's always there,
    My love for you.

FOREVER US

"Alone" is a word
    That appeals to me never.
"Us" is our concept,
    Our feeling forever.

Time has a strange
    And magnificent motion.
Love is the meaning—
    The tide in this ocean.

Each individual
    Struggles to find
A partner in body,
    A match for the mind.

My searching is over—
    Love's tide has pulled in.
Now is the moment
    For time to begin.

Time is our ally—
    Life's so appealing.
We're locked through the ages
    Forever in feeling.

Hope is our candle;
    Love is our guide.
Our hearts say "forever us"
    Deep down inside.

YOU AND I

You and I,
    A special phrase,
That warms the night
    And lights the days.

You and I,
    A concept true,
That speaks of love
    And visions new.

You and I,
    A precious time,
A gentle thought,
    A tender rhyme.

You and I,
    Two hearts that care,
Two minds that mesh,
    Two lives that share.

Love and hope
    And sun and sky
Now whisper dreams
    Of you and I.

YOU ARE MY STAR

You are my star
    Shining ever so bright.
You walk with the sun;
    You challenge the night.

You guide me through darkness,
    Chase shadows by day.
You force all the problems
    Of living away.

You warm by your presence;
    You lift up my moods.
You raise me in spirit
    To high altitudes.

You light up my thinking;
    You charm every hour.
You summon within me
    A much higher power.

You color my future,
    Cast rainbows afar.
You're my stellar body—
    Yes, you are my star.

YOU'RE PERFECT IN MY EYES

Like clouds across the sunset,
    A moon in starry skies,
A rainfall in the springtime—
    You're perfect in my eyes.

All beauty has its shades and tones,
    Each gem a form that's raw.
Each diamond has a subtle way
    Of mirroring its flaw.

I see you as the misty mask
    Enshrouding early day.
I see you as the wildflower
    Nuzzling grass away.

I see you as a naked form
    With memory's lonely scars.
I see you as a feeling
    That no inner knowledge mars.

I see you as temptation
    Casting off your scant disguise.
I see you as a natural—
    You're perfect in my eyes.

THE FLOWER

An understated majesty
    In every flower grows.
In humankind the blossoming
    Of souls through kindness shows.

Examples sown by others
    Soon press through our soil of deeds.
The sprouting of compassion
    Draws its light from human needs.

The stand of our humanity
    Extends its slender reach.
The forming buds attest our growth,
    Potential filling each.

And in the spring of giving,
    In the moisture of concern,
The flower lets its dignity
    Unfold, its colors burn.

How often is the ground prepared,
    Examples softly sown,
And flowers fail to blossom,
    Stems of caring scarcely grown?

Yet hallowed is the moment,
    Which in some forever looms,
When love unfolds its canopy
    And, softly sharing, blooms.

DEAR LOVE

If I could read my heart to you,
  Reveal it line by line,
And capture all the feelings
  I've been trying to define,

I'd describe an endless flow
  Of positive emotions;
Page by page I'd pour to you
  My purest of devotions.

And as my letter rushed along
  As freely as a brook,
I would let my inspirations
  Turn into a book.

Then as my loving words disclosed
  The depths of my affection
And just one book was not enough,
  I'd author a collection.

But since I can't keep up with all
  The feelings of my heart,
I'll have to let this simple page
  My heartfelt story start.

OF A FEATHER

Plumage shared
    In snow-filled weather,
Birds in forest
    Of a feather.

Hopping lightly,
    Softly bounding,
Chase each other
    Without sounding.

Lost in life,
    They bounce along,
Immersed in selves,
    Avoiding song;

As you and I
    Emote like birds,
Rich in senses,
    Free of words,

Floating softly,
    Deep emotions,
In our love's
    Adjacent oceans.

YOU ARE MY PEACE

You are all the quiet moments
    Life has given me.
You're the soft and taming force
    That stills the seething sea.

You're the breath of healing warmth
    Subduing breezes cold.
You're the years of happiness
    That challenge growing old.

You're the antidote for pain,
    The salve for my emotions.
You're the vast expanse of love
    As infinite as oceans.

You're the joy of forests green,
    The miracle of mountains.
You are nature to my thoughts,
    A brook of gushing fountains.

You're the warming rain of spring,
    The brightest hues of fall.
You repel my solitude
    When loneliness is all.

You have filled my sky with wonder
    Like a flight of geese.
You have helped my heart
    To understand the concept peace.

Love's Companionship

I'M FEELING CLOSE TO YOU

A message inside me,
    A feeling I know
Is stirring a warm
    And affectionate glow.

I'm feeling so close to you,
    Feeling so near,
That songs from my heart
    Are all that I hear.

Your spirit has drifted
    Right into my dreams.
I'm endlessly seeing
    Your image, it seems.

Our hearts are together;
    Our spirits are free;
We're drifting together
    So effortlessly.

No distance, no freedom
    Can draw us apart.
I'm closer to you where it counts—
    In the heart.

IF MY HEART COULD TALK

If my heart and mind could capture
    Feelings that I know
And speak them plainly,
    All the things I want to say would flow.

But I can never seem to find
    The phrases that I seek
To tell you softly everything
    My heart would like to speak.

Emotions resting in the heart
    Sustain and feed the soul.
Your presence in my life just seems
    To make my spirit whole.

But I cannot explain the thoughts
    That filter through my day.
Your meaning is much more to me
    Than words can ever say.

PROTECTIVE SPIRITS

I kept guard over you
    In my thoughts,
Feeling that you were safer
    When you were close to my day.

It wasn't a conscious act
    Of remembering that kept you there,
Just the simple fact that
    When we're not together,
        We're not truly apart.

Your tender touch upon my time
    Wings me through my day,
Gliding me through routine moments
    With soft millisecond glimpses
        Into the shelter of your countenance.

Strange that the protective spirit
    I maintain for you
Seems to reflect your presence
    Back into my day
        And offer me comfort and security.

I hope your day benefits as mine,
    Being a little less lonely,
Feeling a little safer, a little more secure,
    By knowing that you're my heart's concern...
        And also my heart's solace.

THOUGHTS OF YOU AND ME

Today I thought
    Of you and me
In morning mists
    Of reverie.

I carried you
    Through later hour
In passing sun
    And warming shower.

I brought you
    To observe my day
And hoped that
    In my thoughts you'd stay.

With people
    And in solitude,
I found you sharing
    Every mood.

And after all
    Was done and said,
Your heart in tow
    Put mine to bed.

WHERE IN THE HEART?

Where in the heart do I find you?
   Where in the mind do you rest?
Where in the focus of springtime
   Do we join in one beautiful quest?

Where in the steep path of living
   Do our patterns of life overlap?
Where in the course of our caring
   Do we journey without any map?

Where in the realm of our senses
   Do we merge into one vital form?
Where in the moments of hardship
   Do we challenge together the storm?

Where in a passionate worldly embrace
   Does our consciousness soar high above?
In the ever mysterious bondage,
   That freedom of spirit called love.

WITH YOU, I'M ME

With you I feel that I can be
    Spontaneous and free.
I open up my heart to you
    In simple honesty.

I share with you my inner thoughts,
    Abandon all disguises.
I bare my deepest feelings,
    Shunning pretense or surprises.

I stand before you as I am,
    My strengths and flaws revealed.
No attitudes are hidden;
    No motives are concealed.

With you I'm free to be myself,
    Voice my identity.
I draw from you an inner calm
    That says—with you, I'm me.

WE NEED EACH OTHER

There's a simple mathematics,
    So absolute and true,
That says that one and one will always
    End up being two.

But there's another set of laws
    With love and life its source
That says two lives together
    Can unleash a vital force.

I know that we have found this force—
    Our spirits truly blend.
We've tapped an inner freedom—
    On each other we depend.

We've found that special meaning—
    We can cherish every hour.
We've discovered our own formula,
    Revealed an inner power—

That chemistry of sharing,
    That higher math of hearts
Whose sum of total being
    Is much greater than its parts.

THANKS FOR LOVING ME

My life was once a game of chance,
  A solitary quest,
A lonely search for someone
  Who could fill my world the best.

But then my heart discovered
  Something pure and something free:
The love I felt for you
  And all that you expressed for me.

You were the substance of my dreams
  So softly coming true.
You saw as much within my soul
  As I perceived in you.

It's sometimes hard to love
  Unless another feels the same.
You let the sparks of true affection
  Mirror back a flame.

When love fills one, it may remain
  A possibility.
When love fills two, dreams can come true—
  So, thanks for loving me.

WE HAVE EACH OTHER

We may at times feel lacking in
   The luxuries of living,
But luxuries cannot compare
   With all that life is giving.

We have our lives together;
   We have our shared affection;
We have the hopes and aspirations
   Of a shared direction.

We have the riches of the heart,
   Of family and friends.
We have respect for one another
   That our loving lends.

We have the comfort of just knowing
   That someone is near.
We have the reassurance
   Of a sympathetic ear.

We have the bounties of each day,
   Events both large and small.
Through all the moments that we share,
   We really have it all.

I'M SECURE IN YOU

There are things the heart won't question,
    Sensations so secure,
That they exist in mind and flesh,
    In primal regions pure.

They have the strength of granite,
    The softness of a touch,
The full persuasion of a flower,
    The warmth that means so much.

I cannot take for granted
    That such treasures are my due.
Instead I'm awed and thankful
    That I feel secure in you.

Such chemistry does not result
    From feeble fascination.
It's active; it's dynamic;
    It needs loving affirmation.

The confidence I feel in you
    Is my profoundest praise.
My love for you will thrive in me
    And brighten all my days.

THANKS FOR ALWAYS BEING THERE

The world is moving faster now—
    We're on a changing course.
But you have helped me deal with life—
    You've been a stable force.

When I have had to follow
    New directions, you were there.
When the world was hard on me,
    You always seemed to care.

When nothing held together,
    Made the slightest bit of sense,
You have always helped restore
    My inner confidence.

Everyone needs someone
    Who's reliable and true.
Through the moments I've endured,
    I'm grateful there was you.

OUR RELATIONSHIP IS SPECIAL

Our relationship is special;
    Our friendship is the best.
Our love is ever growing;
    Our life's a wondrous quest.

We share all things together;
    We never feel alone.
We look at all we've been through;
    We look at how we've grown.

We grasp the tender moments,
    The times we spend as one.
We savor our accomplishments,
    The projects we've begun.

We think of how much better
    Life flows as you and me.
We can't escape the loving thought
    That we were meant to be.

I BELIEVE IN US

I believe in thoughts we share,
In feelings we discuss.
I believe in magic moments—
I believe in us.

I believe in sunny days,
The warming touch of rain.
I believe in special times
That form an endless chain.

I believe in quiet nights,
In vivid starlit skies.
I believe in tender sights
That stir romantic eyes.

I believe in positives,
In truths that form a plus.
I believe in love and sharing—
I believe in us.

I'LL NEVER KNOW ANOTHER YOU

You bring me out—
    You hear my soul.
With you I'm real—
    I play no role.

My talk is true—
    My thoughts are free.
I find myself
    In you and me.

It's hard to find
    A closer two.
I'll never know
    Another you.

There is no better
    Way to show
The way I think,
    The way I grow

Than in those candid
    Times we choose
To trade our feelings,
    Share our views—

The moments deep,
    The moments fair,
The times we open up
    To care.

LOVING YOU

Loving you is all I ask for.
    Loving you is life's reward.
Loving you keeps life in balance.
    Loving you, I'm never bored.

Loving you makes day inviting.
    Loving you makes sharing fun.
Loving you makes absence harder.
    Loving you brings out the sun.

Loving you makes hope much stronger.
    Loving you makes dreaming real.
Loving you is thought sufficient.
    Loving you is what I feel.

Loving you is built on caring,
    All my lonely feelings stilled.
Loving you is where my heart is.
    Loving you is wish fulfilled.

A DAY WITH YOU

A day with you
    Is more to me
Than any miracle
    Of spring,

Than any sun
    That paints the sky,
Than any song
    That wants to sing.

A day with you
    Will lift me up
And hold me close
    When I am down

And make me special
    When I'm not
And touch my spirits
    Like a crown.

A day with you
    Is rich in caring,
More than any dream
    Can say;

And just the hope
    Of our tomorrow
Makes a gift
    Of my today.

Cozy Love

I NEED A HUG

At the end of a lengthy
    And tiring day
When I've faced the world
    In my private way,
                I need a hug!

When I'm hungry and cranky
    And feeling up tight
And a day has just passed
    When too little went right,
                I need a hug!

When my body is craving
    The warmth of another
And my poor aching muscles
    Compete with each other,
                I need a hug!

When I'm insecure
    And a little bit nutty
And my mind is exhausted,
    My body like putty,
                I need a hug!

When I am affectionate,
    Loving and caring
And want to enjoy
    A real moment of sharing,
                I need a hug!

YOU WARM UP MY TOES

You warm my feet,
   Revive my toes;
You cure my chilly
   Bedtime woes.

You make the dark
   Fill up with light.
You make a comfy
   Place of night.

You touch me softly,
   Nuzzle, press
And chase away
   My loneliness.

I feel your form
   As part of mine.
As we reach out,
   Our hearts combine.

Your slumber stirs
   A loving laugh
When you sprawl out
   And hog my half.

And I drink in
   Our warmth as lovers,
Though you at times
   Grab all my covers.

BREATH OF NIGHT

You fell asleep before me—
    Now you drift in upward breezes.
You're like a seed borne into flight
    That each new current teases.

Your peace in free fall slumber
    Lifts you up into the sky.
Your breath propels you further
    As you slip into a sigh.

I feel your warming presence
    As I watch your spirit soar.
I sense the upper reaches
    You so earnestly explore.

I see the gentle air on which
    You float without a frown
And hope the winds of freedom
    Will softly set you down.

A QUIET KISS GOOD NIGHT

Sometimes love is simple
    In its needs,
Existing with no call for
    Special deeds.

The nighttime stillness
    Of two nesting birds
Is shared in us when we
    Relinquish words.

We lie in quiet moments
    Side by side
Allowing but our presence
    To provide.

And then to warm the shadows
    With our light,
Our lips search out
    A quiet kiss good night.

SILENCE SHARED

Listening to silence,
    We sat in the distilled quiet
    Of our thoughts.
We didn't mind the empty moments
    And didn't try to fill them.

Our free associations dashed
    In unguarded randomness,
Unweighted by guilt,
    Unmoved by lost conversation.

This freedom not to talk,
    This comfort in each other,
Signed with sealed lips
    A statement about love
That justified any idle words
    We may have missed.

COME CLOSE TO ME

Come close to me,
　　Lie warm to warm,
　　　　Attend my pulse,
　　　　　　Appease my heart.

Excuse the world,
　　Dismiss the loud,
　　　　Reject the rude,
　　　　　　Away with all.

Erase alone,
　　Retire fear,
　　　　Dispel the hurt,
　　　　　　Release the sad.

Emerge as one,
　　Complete the whole,
　　　　Acquire peace,
　　　　　　Embrace the calm.

DAY OF NIGHT

The deck is lit
　　With moonlight,
The day of night
　　Presiding.

We face our windowed doors
　　From bed
In quilted comfort
　　Hiding.

We listen to the
　　Noises
As the chilly winds
　　Rush by.

We fit together,
　　Trading warmth,
As front to back
　　We lie.

I ride my hand
　　Around your form,
As sight and sound
　　And feel

Collaborate
　　In harmony
The wintry cold
　　To heal.

HARDLY RAIN

It rained that day
      But in the damp
            That early May supplied
I knew despite
      The chill of droplets
            There was sun inside.

The skies were blind
      To rays above—
            The clouds effused their tears;
But all that you
      Imply to me
            The darkest moment clears.

So even as I heard
      The splashing cadence
            Of the day,
I saw the sun
      Within your heart
            And couldn't feel the gray.

MORNING MUSIC

Soloist dove,
    You relax
        The morning frenzy
Of stirring crows
    And cars
        Racing to work.

You enter a near-duet
    With available other,
Randomly overlapping notes,
    Teasing music and togetherness
        From the early hour,
Tempting togetherness
    In us.

You drift into quiet,
    Solidifying ours
As we embrace the morning
    In peaceful after-sleep...
        After us.

Light Love

LEND ME LOVE

Lend me love
  And love me true
And lure me into
  Debt with you.

All the love that
  I can borrow
I'll repay before
  Tomorrow.

To the sum of
  Totals due
I'll add my highest
  Interest, too.

That way my payments
  Will accrue
As functions of
  My love for you.

Each time your heart
  Approves a loan,
I'll reimburse it
  From my own.

I'M CRAZY OVER YOU

Sometimes I'm crazy, distracted, confounded
    And climbing the walls over you.
No matter the season, the day or the reason,
    These feelings I just can't subdue.

I'm babbling, billowing, bubbling over—
    I'm feeling berserk and unstable.
I can't get a grip on myself or my feelings—
    When I try to calm down, I'm unable.

I'm out of this world with excitement.
    I'm feeling mixed up through and through.
I'm high in the sky and I'm crazy—
    I'm wildly insane about you.

I LOVE YOUR MYSTERY

You're rather unpredictable;
    You're different, not the same—
A puzzle to decipher,
    A freest wind to tame.

I never hope to understand
    Your subtleties and shades.
Each time I chase your meaning,
    All my comprehension fades.

I never can predict exactly
    How you're going to act.
The only thing that's constant
    Is the way that you attract.

I'll never find the answers—
    All solutions you defy.
But since I love your mystery,
    It's fun for me to try.

I NEED A LITTLE YOU

I need a little you
   To make the day a little brighter.
I need a little you
   To make my duties seem much lighter.

I need a little you
   To help me see life's faults and face them.
I need a little you
   To take my problems and erase them.

I need a little you
   To want to share my company.
I need a little you
   To need a little bit of me.

I need a little you
   To draw so close that I can squeeze you.
I need a little you,
   Because I want the chance to please you.

I need a little you
   So I have someone to adore.
I need a little you,
   But I could really use much more.

DOING IT WITH YOU

Life has many details
    And assorted tasks to do,
But everything is richer
    If I'm doing it with you.

Every simple routine
    Making up an average day
Turns into a special gift
    When shared in our own way.

Every passing moment
    Has its color and its tone,
But life is more rewarding
    Spent with you and not alone.

Life may ration its rewards,
    Give recognitions few,
But life will always soar
    When it is generous with you.

YOU LIGHT UP MY FIRE

Love is a part of my mind
    That goes crazy,
Summoning, seeking
    An image of you.

Love is a silly thought
    Waking my body,
Shimmering, shivering
    All through and through.

Love's a connection,
    A pulling together,
A union of kindness,
    A harvest of feeling.

Love is a spirit that
    Tickles and teases
And lights up my fires
    In ways so appealing.

Love is the thought of you
    Riding beside me,
Keeping me company
    All through the day.

Love is the luscious excitement
    You bring me,
Stirring my life
    In a wonderful way.

Our Love

WE WERE MEANT TO BE

Certain chance occurrences
    Have caused our paths to meet.
Destiny has joined our hearts
    And made our lives complete.

Not all lives that cross
    Produce a union that is strong.
Fate can sometimes tempt
    And then remind us we were wrong.

Fortune has confirmed
    Our love is not a false disguise.
Love is something we in time
    Will truly maximize.

Something rare has happened—
    Life has given us a chance.
There is something natural
    And true in our romance.

Days are so delicious—
    Time is special; minds are free.
I believe our love is real
    And we were meant to be.

THE FORCE OF TWO

My love for you is part of me—
    It leads me through each day.
It blends with every conscious thought
    And softly shows the way.

It frees me from concern
    And gives my dreams a tender base.
Whenever you are near,
    The world is easier to face.

My love for you completes
    The highest circle of my heart
And tells me that your role
    Has turned into a leading part.

You give my deeper feelings
    And my warmth a place to grow.
You lift my spirits to the sky,
    Release an inner glow.

Your love allows my passions
    To explore the force of two
And redefines in countless precious ways
    My love for you.

I LOVE YOU

I'm thinking, dreaming,
    Conscious of you,
Feeling, knowing
    That I love you.

I'm sensing, seeing
    How you haunt me,
Wishing, hoping
    That you want me.

I'm noting, minding
    How I heed you,
Contemplating
    That I need you.

I'm witnessing
    Through waves and oceans
How you govern
    My emotions.

No thought I have
    Exists above you.
In my heart I know
    I love you.

LOVE IS...

Love is finding that with you
    Each simple thing is something new,
Each winter hour is full of spring,
    Each moment is worth cherishing.

It's feeling in your presence free
    And knowing that with you I'm me.
It's finding comfort at your side
    And seeking moments to confide.

It's sensing darkness when you're gone
    Yet knowing night must yield to dawn.
It's feeling snug when we're together
    And finding calm in any weather.

It's feeling youth at every age.
    It's being rich despite your wage.
It's feeling happy, seldom blue;
    But, darling, most of all it's you!

ALL I WANT IS YOU

I'll tell it rather simply;
    I'll say it plain and true—
A single thing is all I want;
    And all I want is you.

There are no other riches,
    No treasures or possessions
That ever could compare with you,
    My fondest of obsessions.

You are the very air I breathe,
    The ration that sustains me.
You're all my thoughts tied up as one,
    The laugh that entertains me.

You're all that life need ever give,
    The maximum that's due.
If I could ask for anything,
    I'd only ask for you.

THE PERFECT TWO

If I define the number *two,*
    There's just one meaning, me and you.
If I explain the pronoun *we,*
    I'm struck with thoughts of you and me.
If I explore the small word *us,*
    I see it lasting ever thus.
If I reflect on life *together,*
    I see no hint of stormy weather.

If there's a chance you share my view
    And see in us the perfect *two*
And feel quite free
    In using *we*
And give a plus
    To dreams of *us,*
Then possibly heart's fragile tether
    Will keep the two of us *together.*

OUR LOVE

Our love is something we have built
    From passions, hopes and dreams.
It's safe from any passing moods,
    Secure from all extremes.

It's something real and special,
    Something solid, something pure.
It's something we can always count on,
    Ringing sound and sure.

It's something grounded in the heart,
    Emitting confidence.
It lives in our emotions;
    It is something we can sense.

Our love remains a binding force,
    Resistant to all strife.
Amidst the outer pressures,
    It's our anchor throughout life.

YOU ARE MY CONSTANT

You are my constant, my
  Count on you
    Care for me
      There for me
        Constant,

My favor me
  Fathom me
    Fight for me
      Constant,

My turn me on
  Urge me on
    Learn my heart
      Constant,

My greet my gaze
  Fill my days
    Brightest rays
      Constant.

You are my
  Singing of
    Stars above
      Endless love
        Constant.

THE ONE I LOVE

The one I love is all I need
    To set my heart ablaze.
The one I love's the center of
    My life in many ways.

The one I love is part of me,
    Companion to my dreams,
And is the main ingredient
    In all my thoughts, it seems.

The one I love supports me through
    The challenges I face
And knows the healing power
    Of a warm and fond embrace.

The one I love responds to me,
    My spirits can renew.
The one I love is full of passion;
    The one I love is you!

REAL DEAL

I wear my inside outside,
    Unabashed in front of you.
I'm not aware of being there—
    I'm worn instead of new.

I'm altogether real to you—
    I'm felt instead of viewed.
I bare my inner being,
    Let you into every mood.

I have no sly exterior,
    No fiction I affect.
I have no false appearance,
    No candor I neglect.

I'm all of me revealed to you,
    An aptitude of we.
I open up as you disclose
    The very same to me.

YOU ARE MY SOULMATE

Your flesh and mine
　　Will share today
And hear what only
　　Hearts can say—

That you are me
　　And I am you
And we are one form
　　Passing through.

I'm in your mind;
　　You're in my soul;
We share one pulse;
　　We fill one role.

The world is vast—
　　Our time is small.
This moment, in the end,
　　Is all.

We'll guard our space,
　　Embrace our dreams,
Enjoy the heat
　　Of passion's themes.

Our spirits joined
　　Are bright and free.
Our love will light
　　Eternity.

COME WHAT MAY

Come what may,
    We joined our hearts,
    We played our parts
        For but a day.

Come what may,
    We lived it well,
    So much to tell
        In our own way.

Come what may,
    We filled our time
    And found it prime
        In work or play.

Come what may,
    We knew this blend
    Some day would end
        And couldn't stay.

Come what may,
    Our passions past
    Would ever last
        Beyond their day.

Come what may,
    The world could sigh
    At our blue sky
        Against its gray.

YOU ARE MY EVERYTHING

As the world is
   Rushing by us,
As the moment
   Hurries on,

You are my
   Entire reason—
You are my
   Untiring dawn.

In a time of
   Choice and changes,
In our struggle
   To exist,

You are all
   That I require—
You're the thought
   I can't resist.

You ignite
   My inner fire.
You make up
   My hopes and dreams.

You are everything
   I need
To love and live through
   Life's extremes.

LET'S STAY YOUNG

Let's stay young
    As we grow old.
Let's find a path
    Between the years.

Let's steer a course
    Of hope and wonder,
Navigate
    The joys and tears.

Let's lift each other
    Over hills—
Have strength for
    Deepest valleys, too.

Let's find a place
    Where dreams live on,
Where we can both
    Enjoy the view.

Let's seek out beauty
    In the present,
Savor times
    Of calm and peace.

Let's love and live,
    Grow old together
While our youth
    Renews its lease.

WHAT LOVE

What love will fill
   This flask of time
And, through your care,
   Improve, like wine?
              . . . Mine.

What love will I
   Consume till high
To stir emotions
   My heart stores?
              . . . Yours.

What love will cross
   Your lips and mine
And free affection's
   Deepest powers?
              . . . Ours.

WHAT IS LOVE?

The glue that holds
    The world together,
The ship that navigates
    All weather,
The wind that lifts us
    Like a feather
              Is love.

The caring that achieves
    Great height,
The way that darkness
    Lets in light,
The vision that
    Exceeds all sight
              Is love.

The knowledge that
    All hopes are one,
The faith that beckons
    Like the sun,
The sea to which
    All rivers run
              Is love.

The dream that motivates
    Each day,
The only goal,
    The brightest ray,
The precious gift
    For which we pray
        Is love.

Love Makes It Work

I'M LOSING SLEEP OVER YOU

Sometimes when I go to bed
    And try in every way
To get a decent night of rest,
    Forget a tiring day,

I discover I'm not drifting
    Into slumber deep—
I'm just staring at the ceiling
    Wishing I could sleep.

You are very often why
    I miss my bedtime cues.
Thoughts of you account for almost
    All the sleep I lose.

I am so aware of you
    That when I sleep it seems
You occupy and heighten
    My most satisfying dreams.

But when it seems I'm lacking
    Just the right amount of you,
Sleeping is the exercise
    My mind won't let me do.

LOVE IS A WORD

Love is a word
   With a sensible sound,
Yet its use makes a sensible
   Head go around.

For it seems that this word
   Can have multiple uses
Which sometimes can lead
   To more subtle abuses.

This says to a sensitive,
   Critical heart
That the language of love
   Is a language apart.

The use of the word
   Affords no real assurance
That the feeling behind it
   Has chance of endurance.

So love can't depend
   On an audible sound,
For the silence of love
   Is a silence profound;

And the actions that help
   In defining this word
Go beyond any message
   So easily heard.

I'M SENSITIVE TO YOU

I'm influenced in many ways
  By things you say and do.
I guess, to put it simply,
  I am sensitive to you.

This means that deep inside my heart
  I've made a conscious choice
To weigh your words with care
  And know each nuance of your voice.

This is the highest compliment,
  The truest sign of love.
It shows that as I live my life
  You're what I'm thinking of.

In giving you complete and total
  Access to my heart,
I focus in on certain feelings
  You alone impart.

This means your words will always have
  A powerful effect.
I may react to things you say
  In ways you don't expect.

I hope that you will understand
  We have so much to share.
If ever I react to you,
  It's just because I care.

LOVE WILL FIND A WAY

Two people can feel very close,
    Their honest love proclaim,
Yet also know that they're free spirits,
    Not at all the same.

Such people need a little room
    To let their spirits speak.
They can't suppress the differences
    That make them so unique.

Freedom exercised with taste
    Can help two people grow.
It helps them understand themselves,
    Lets deeper talents show.

Though two may give each other space,
    No loss of love's to blame,
For they have merely recognized
    They're different, not the same.

A positive conclusion
    Is much easier to assume
When two have found enough respect
    To give each other room.

LOVE MAKES IT WORK

We needn't pretend that it's perfect,
    Nor dwell on the fact that it's not.
We needn't expect a relationship
    Devoid of all blemish or spot.

It's normal to be a bit human:
    Some problems are part of the game.
Things would be hopelessly boring
    If, flawlessly, we were the same.

But still it's important to notice,
    No matter how human we are,
That love is the measure of progress:
    It leads us and guides us afar.

We don't have to worship perfection,
    Nor give up all struggle for change;
But love can be perfect when we're not—
    It's a gift we can proudly exchange.

PLEASE SAVE SOME TIME FOR ME

The time we share has grown too scarce;
    Our special moments flee.
Though life has its required tasks,
    Please save some time for me.

There are so many routine things
    To occupy our days
It's often hard to meet within
    The center of our maze.

We give a lot of extra effort
    To the things we do
And often spend our energies
    Alone and not as two.

And when our first free moment
    Then becomes a date to keep,
Our need to share competes with our
    More basic need for sleep.

My batteries need charging;
    I'm short of energy.
I want to share my life with you—
    Please save some time for me.

IF YOU HAD SAID GOOD NIGHT

You left me to myself
    And to the thoughts that I was facing.
Your breath and body slowed to sleep—
    My heart and mind were racing.

I couldn't stand to be alone
    Without a moment's parting.
Your day was winding down
    And yet my night was sadly starting.

I needed someone's softness
    To adjourn my day to dreaming.
You slipped away so quietly
    Your silence left me steaming.

I wish that you had sensed
    My simple need for interaction
And didn't leave me all alone
    To fight the night's distraction.

My lonely state of mind,
    Intent on darkness, craved your light.
It would have been much easier
    If you had said good night.

LET'S COMMUNICATE

Let's never underestimate
    Our power to communicate.
If pressures lead to words unfair,
    Let's talk it over, clear the air.
If dialogue can save the day,
    Let's seek the words and find a way.
If inner thoughts are stirring doubt,
    Let's care enough to talk it out.
So silence cannot barriers build,
    Let's keep our lives discussion-filled.
So we don't burst with things unsaid,
    Let's practice speaking out instead.
So we can both feel good inside,
    Let's know we always can confide.
So tender thoughts don't slip the mind,
    Let's always share a word that's kind.
So love is nourished day by day,
    Let's speak our hearts in every way.

LET'S MAKE IT WORK

Our relationship is strong enough
    To weather any test.
With conscious effort we can strive
    To make our love the best.

If we can only empathize
    With one another's feelings
And learn to talk out differences
    Without our thoughts concealing,

We'll prove that in those periods
    Of tensions overflowing
Our hearts are patient through it all—
    Our love is ever growing.

If we can stress the positive,
    Not magnify the worst,
We'll focus on each other's strengths
    And see the good things first.

If we can see the brighter side
    Through every shade of weather,
We'll have the confidence to say:
    Let's make it work together.

LOVE HURTS

Love can change you,
  Rearrange you,
Send you bliss
  Within a kiss;
But when it leaves you
  Or deceives you,
When emotions
  Storm like oceans,
    Love hurts.

When you're sharing,
  Always caring,
Life is flowing,
  Hearts are glowing,
Dreams are surer,
  Feelings purer,
Till dissension
  Leads to tension, then
    Love hurts.

Love brings hope
  And helps you cope,
But love's despair
  Defies repair;
And all of reason
  Has no season;
And wisdom's laws
  Won't help, because
    Love hurts.

LOVE-LESSON

Love is easy
    To question—
It's built on a soft
    Bed of feelings.

It's rooted in gestures
    Of tenderness,
Awareness that helps
    With its healings.

Its base may be parched
    With confusion;
Its hopes may be hurt
    By despair;

Its joy may have lost
    Understanding;
Its spirit may struggle
    For air.

But a sprinkle of small things
    Will moisten
And slowly revive
    Moods of caring;

And hearts will look forward
    Together
With patience and passion
    And sharing.

Endless Love

MARRIAGE OF TWO HEARTS

In every heart there is a spark
    That wants to be a flame.
In every life there is a part
    That only love can tame.

In every day there is a moment
    Eager to be shared.
In every mind a tender thought
    Just waits to be declared.

In every forest there's a trail
    Which two can happier roam.
In every place there is a spot
    Which two can call a home.

In every joy a higher gladness
    Reigns if there are two.
In every love there is the hope
    That dreams will all come true.

In every marriage of two hearts
    Two lives exist as one.
In every journey that two share
    Life's really just begun.

LOVE IS ALWAYS THERE

The life we lead,
   The hopes we share
Remind us love
   Is always there.

When roads we walk
   Appear uphill,
We demonstrate
   A patient will.

When life's dilemmas
   Pass us by,
We celebrate
   A cloudless sky.

The dullest trip
   Would always be
On flattest land
   Or quiet sea.

But how enchanting
   Is the quest
That sometimes puts us
   To the test.

And how exciting
   Is the find
When lives are fondly
   Intertwined.

MY WIFE, MY LOVE

My wife, my love, my dearest friend,
    You've given me your heart to tend.
I've given you my life to share;
    My heart is in your tender care.

My wife, my hope, my fondest dream,
    We form a true devoted team.
In all the moments life may bring,
    You are my star, my everything.

My wife, my source of lasting truth,
    You stir in me eternal youth;
You give my heart a sense of pride;
    You fuel my warmest thoughts inside.

My wife, my daily inspiration,
    You're the love in my equation.
You're my source of deep affection.
    You're my compass and direction.

THE MESSAGE OF OUR MARRIAGE

The message of our marriage
    Started softly with a kiss.
The meaning of the moment
    Spoke a truth we couldn't miss.

The fact about the future
    Was that you and I were one.
The loneliness and isolation
    Of the past were done.

The ritual of joining
    Hearts together left us shining.
We traded vows of hope and trust,
    Through love our souls combining.

Our rings embraced commitment,
    Circled lives, let spirits mend.
Upon our fingers they inscribed
    A future without end.

The promise of together
    Left a treasure for tomorrow.
The warmth of you and me became
    A strength from which to borrow.

HAPPY BIRTHDAY, SWEETHEART

This day was meant for you, my love—
    You're all that I am thinking of.
There's nothing I would rather do
    Than spend this special time with you.

Your birthday will fond memories fill;
    But in our feelings time stands still.
Our life together turns a page;
    But in our hearts love has no age.

Togetherness is our true vow—
    We're living in a sacred now.
We value all the things we share—
    Our perfect space is everywhere.

This birthday wish tells how I feel—
    My love for you is very real.
It seems the proper time to say—
    I love you, dear, in every way.

ANNIVERSARY OF OUR LOVE

Let's recall that moment
　　When our love had just begun,
That special place in time
　　When all our hopes were joined as one.

Let us now reflect upon
　　The precious past we feel,
The tender anniversary
　　Our hearts embrace as real.

Let's remember all that happened
　　In our lives that day
To send a deeper message
　　Of devotion that would stay.

Let's affirm that all we know
　　Of love and true affection
Started flowing when our dreams
　　Assumed the same direction.

And now as I look back
　　At how our early passions grew,
I celebrate and cherish
　　My discovery of you.

TILL THE END OF TIME

I'll love you till
    The end of time.
I'll love you with
    My total being.

I'll cherish you
    In thought and touch.
I'll cherish every
    Moment fleeing.

I'll pull your spirit
    Into mine.
I'll press my heartbeat
    Into yours.

I'll care for you
    With patient love.
I'll follow you
    To distant shores.

I'll join with you
    In every way.
I'll share as much
    As I can give.

I'll love you with
    Forever's promise,
Love that will
    This life outlive.

LOVE ACROSS TIME

Love has one dimension
    That's beyond both time and space.
No amount of living
    Can this vital force erase.

The heart preserves a dialog,
    A unity of spirit,
That taps the beauty of the past
    And keeps you always near it.

You remain the eyes and ears,
    The pulse of one you love.
Thoughts comprise an open dream
    To one you're thinking of.

Two minds that fuse in consciousness
    Become the same as one.
The link that love provides through time
    Can never be undone.

All the things that cross your heart
    And you would like to share
Are telegraphed in spirit
    To the love that's always there.

MORNING IDYLL

As we press close
  And chase away
    Morning's early chill,
The lifting fog
  Beyond our door
Uncovers the warm,
  Distant sound
    Of a dove,
Invisibly occupying
  Its usual perch
    In our consciousness.

The comforting, almost unearthly,
  Mourning sound
    Calms our souls,
Pauses time with its
  Timelessness,
Rewards years
  Of quiet listening.

A simple refrain—
  Over the mist,
    Over our melted forms,
      Over the arousal of day—
Plumbs our depths,
  Our pasts,
Up to and including—
  Even after—
    You and me.

OUR LOVE IS YOUNG

Our love is young
    When in the morning dew
I grasp the day
    Through eye-moist pools of you.

Our love is young
    When I compose a tear
At times when you are
    Far away, not near.

Our love is young
    When passions still are bold
And you're the only dream
    I wish to hold.

Our love is young
    When all our days are dear
And even in the clouds
    Our view is clear.

Our love is young
    When gems of time we sort
And memories forever
    Seem too short.

Our love is young
    And hearts are warm, not cold,
When feelings still are new
    Though life grows old.

THE TOUCH OF LOVE

Toe to toe we link
  In weather hot.
We sprawl about and fill
  Our sleeping spot.

The bridge we've built
  Enriches from within.
We are secure
  When summer air comes in.

As winter takes away
  The August warm,
Our bodies crowd together
  And conform.

Embracing or apart
  Our spirits flow—
Our love is more persistent
  Than we know.

It reaches out
  In silence or in smiles.
It penetrates the inches
  Or the miles.

And when a life must
  Turn its final pages,
The awesome touch of love
  Survives the ages.

WE ARE ONE

We are one,
　　Reborn from two.
Life has joined us,
　　Shaped our view.

Sharing is
　　The way we feel.
Tenderness
　　Is our ideal.

Loneliness
　　Defines our past.
Now our warmth
　　Is meant to last.

All the world
　　Was split in two;
Now we're whole—
　　One body true.

Time was fractured;
　　Time was lost;
Time was chilled
　　In winter frost.

Now the ages
　　Have our trust,
And dreams and hopes
　　Won't fade to dust.

Familiar Love

HEART RATE

You follow the moving treads 2.3 miles,
    Alternately walking and running,
Then dismount
    To walk your pulse
      Back to normal
And chill your steamy flesh
    Against dark patches of sweat
      Daubed seductively
        On your grey T-shirt.

Guy-like, you toss your top off
    And field your five-pound weights,
      Facing me with repetitions
        Of lift and curl and stretch.
I gather in your gorgeous,
    Glistening features
And let my laptop screen
    Shift into energy-saver mode,
      While I can't.

Had I thought to google the word "ecstasy,"
    I could not have clicked on
      A better result
Than your 'cool down' routine,
    More real than virtual,
      And cool enough to be searing.

LAST TOUCH OF DAY

Exhaling, exhausted,
　Back meets mattress,
　　And details of day
　　　Plunge to a stop
　　　In one final,
　　　　Relaxing descent.
Gravity pins me
　To bed sheets.
Life de-programs,
　Soft focusing the day
　　And its events.

Suspended between
　Wakefulness and sleep,
　　I coast through the air,
　　　Too weak to lock on a theme.

You are there,
　And I lean over
　　To consummate the day
　　　With my lips upon yours . . .
But I do this
　Only in thought.

Instead of pushing myself up
And twisting my head
To locate yours,
I slide my mid-body
Against your warmth
And move my foot
Alongside yours
So a couple of toes
Can touch.
Somehow, day vanishes
In the stretching fog
Of this moment . . .
And that is all.

METEOR SHOWER

Looking high
    At August sky
We train our gaze
    On chances.

Arcs of light
    In modest flight
Are lost in
    Cloud advances.

But as the stars
    Adorning night
Are freed of
    Blankets gray,

A streak of
    Burning ember
Cuts across
    In brash display.

This blazing trail
    Of wonder
Breezes through
    Our field of dreams,

And since our eyes
     Have shared its path,
How rich
     The moment seems.

And as we stare
     At nothing,
Pulling promise
     From the night,

We ease our forms
     In close
And let our own
     Deep flames ignite.

THE VIEW

The owl piped its eight notes
　　Through our cracked window
　　　And roused us
　　　　To a moonlit song.

I was the first to move,
　　To open the door,
　　　To enter the night,
　　　　As you lay still.

As you lay still,
　　Eyes rode bare flesh
　　　Across chill planks
　　　And waited

Before resuming
　　The holy song...
　　　And the listening.

HEAVY BREATHING

You are this hot sleeping
   Summer body,
Breathing on my bare back,
   Too wonderfully close
     For comfort.

I am propped on my side,
   Facing my 2:00 AM clock,
     Arm and ear hugging
      My soft pillow,
Marking the minutes
   With my own breath.

I monitor your Technicolor dreams
   Through deep, nuanced inhales
     And exhales,
Hoping my own light fantasies
   Will soon flood
     My awareness.

Outdoor insects sleep,
   As screened windows
     Sift silence
      Over our breathing
And let us link worlds
   From there to here
     And back,
       Only inches apart.

PLACE OF WORSHIP

I worship the crickets
　　And the big dipper,
The sounds of a recent rain
　　Dripping in the forest,
The cool fresh air
　　Chilling a summer night,
The porridge fog
　　Slowing up morning,
The bluebird flashing its ocean colors
　　In a green bush,
The wild flowers scattering bouquets
　　In a pasture,
The thoughts of family
　　Across the full spectrum of life,
The seasons whisking by
　　In slow motion,
The gift of renewal and rebirth,
　　Reinforced time and again,
The composting of memory
　　Through loss and change,
The presence of you next to me,
　　Walking, working, and at rest,
In body, mind,
　　And spirit.

SAVE THE NON SEQUITUR

The New York Times
    Was on our kitchen table,
        Relating incidents
            Of global war and strife.
We soberly discussed
    The massacre
        Of 600 civilians
            In Liberia.

That week, the opening of
    Our backyard pool for the season
        Had left our
            Filtration system a mess,
With algae and tree debris
    Clogging our
        Diatomaceous earth filter.

Without transition or introduction,
    My thoughts wandered
        From global conflict
            To household chores.
It was in utter
    Stream of consciousness
That I said
    In casual understatement,
        "Let's change the earth today."

In spontaneous response,
    We both sighed
        And hugged tightly,
            Wishing that such could be the case.

PLAYING IN THE DIRT

As you stand there,
  Trowel in hand,
    About to stir up
      Garden soils,
I see a smaller you,
  Bucket in hand,
    Shovel ready,
Eager to begin
  Your sandbox duties—
    Fillings and emptyings,
      Pilings and movings.

From those imagination-filled
  Villages and dwellings
    To today's fertile enclosures
      For seeds and sprouts,
You inhabit the soil
  With your ideas,
    Invest it with effort,
      Prod its potential.

Home for you feels best
    In the dirt;
And you will come back today,
    Mud-streaked
        And glowing,
Proud of hours spent,
    Offspring prepped and placed,
        Tamped and watered,
Sullied hands clasping
    That special shovel
With its sacred connection
    To something primal
        And far in the past.

BUCKET OF WORMS

This dank March day
    You don your sweats
        And walk our road,
For exercise first,
    Then to rescue stranded worms
        From the damp alluring asphalt.

It hardly evokes the lacy elegance
    You wore down the aisle
        Forty years to the day before.
I'm certain that had I tried
    To preview the decades ahead
        Such prescience
            Would have been impossible.

Needless to say, forty years
    Has educated me to expect
        That an anniversary commemoration
Could easily include several worms
    Deposited into garden and compost pile
        For each of those lovely forty years.

With fond recall, I can flash back
    To moments that March day
When I held your hand
    And walked by your side
        To commence the journey
        We celebrate today.

Easier to think of clasping
    Your hand then, however,
        Than to think of it now,
After you have eased
    The local distressed worm population
        Out of danger
            With your caring hands
And brought them to
    A life of patient toil
        In our garden.

Would that I had the industry
    Of those worms,
        Led and inspired now
            By you, my wife of forty years,
Whose hand, just for the moment,
    I may want to avoid holding.

SLOW DANCING

We held each other
   In the slow dance
      Of our before,
Feeling like kids
   In the newness
      Of old impressions.

Hugging the floor,
   We embraced
      Melodies and words,
Moods guiding
   Our motions.

Our familiar forms
   Still held mystery,
As seasoned steps
   Brushed us close
      Together.

Bodies well known
   To each other
Clung softly
   To the moment;
And the past drifted
   In and out of us
      In affectionate waves,

As time held
    Preciously on
        To us
As if today
    And yesterday
        Were one.

YOUR EYES

Glow pools of yes,
Soft floods of caring,
Glinting beacons of humor,
Bright windows of personality,
Moist messengers of compassion,
Onyx oceans of principle,

Illuminating my life,
Melting my moods,
Building and bursting my bubbles,
Convecting my warmth,
Prodding my passions,
Surprising my senses,
Unleashing my awe,
Sparking my wonder,
Radiating love,
Harnessing mine.

Whimsical Love

BODY SPECIALIST

Your gray, long-sleeved night shirt
   Emblazons the name and comic logo
    Of our local auto body shop,
Incubating you in undercover warmth
   On chill winter nights,
Delivering a multi-year commercial
   For a once-utilized collision specialist.

It reaches just below your panties,
   Allowing your true colors,
    Your leg-high flesh tones,
To follow your bottom's curve
   For the imagination.

The baggy shirt hides your
   Youthful curves
In ways un-guessed by
   Teasing designers at Victoria's Secret,
Hawking their scant, diaphanous
   Sleepwear.

In a peculiar way,
   This bulky, almost unflattering,
    Collision Specialist T-shirt
     Baits me inside
To review with my hands
   And reaffirm for the mind
The details any good body shop
   Could hardly envision
    And couldn't hope to improve.

DISH-PLAY

Decades after the fact,
   Your night shirt flung
      Into adjacent laundry's
         Awaiting top loader,
You work the kitchen,
   Forming flour into dough,
      Filling drainer with dripping dishes,
      Clothed only in thought
         And cotton briefs.

As I glance up
   From my computer monitor,
Your profiled labors
   Turn me helpless,
      Dash my attention
And leave me unable to focus
   On the news column
      I am reading
Or hold my gaze
   To the screen.

Opinions expressed
    Cannot displace fact—
      Your fact—
The fact of decades shared,
    Launched with a formal "I do"
And refined over time
    Into casual, alluring moments
      Of kneading dough
And uninhibited splashes
    At the sink—
      By the only dish I know.

LOVE POEM

We've shoveled snow from
  Driveways and roads,
    Cured sinkholes,
      Thawed water lines,
        Cleared storm drains,
Redirected streams,
  Restored culverts,
    Improved road drainage,
Repaired clocks, music boxes,
  Cars of all sizes,
    An antique Victrola,
Office and production equipment,
  Computers, phones, cables and circuits,
    Faucets, showers, toilets,
Lights, chandeliers
  And ceiling fans,

Plotted our lot's topography,
  Tested soil percolation,
    Designed our first house,
Maintained grass, leaves and gardens
  On estates of all sizes,
    Formed a business or two,
      Moved mountains of memories,
Reveled in new lives emerging,
  Consoled at old lives receding,

Excited to the draw of
    Lithe, unblemished youth,
Carried this fascination
    Into advancing maturity,
Loved intensely through scars
    That cut us
        But hardly changed us,

Explored every trail
    We could find,
Cuddled under night's covers
    And welcomed the touch
        And pulse of morning,
Felt the ecstasy of forms,
    Belly close,
        Intimately connected
In ways imagined
    Through daylong, lifelong fantasies
        Hatched in the gratifying,
        Surprisingly sensual
           Humdrum of it all.

SHOPPING FOR BATHING SUITS

Peeling you in and out of colorful wrappings,
    We shopped bathing suits.
Each opening of the changing room curtain
    Presented a new you.

Suits of different cuts
    Exposed different parts of you,
Highlighted you in different ways—
    Sculpting, revealing, defining
        Breasts or bottom;
Baring, flattering, concealing
    Sides, back, hips and belly.

I watched as florals, solids, stripes and abstracts,
    One-piece and two-piece,
        Flesh-thin and lined,
Spoke your form to me
    And declared it, potentially, to others.

In the half-privacy of your dressing room,
    In the privacy of ourselves,
You tested the fit of tops, bottoms, and tanks
    With indelicate tugs, unguarded pulls,
        And petty disclosures to the mirror.

Your casual disrobing,
   Behind the almost drawn curtain,
      Detailed your form to me in secret showings,
      Rewarding my unplanned glances.
Unselfconsciously you reminded me
   That coverings obscure your true meaning
And succeed only as they allow your
   Natural form through.

The flesh I knew needed nothing
   But to present the bare truth,
Now slipping in and out of concealment,
   One bathing suit after another.

It didn't need to be shaped, formed, uplifted,
   Rearranged or defined in fashion or color,
But rather needed only the reality of its own tint,
   The contour of its own silhouette unchanged,
      And the covering of a private moment shared.

PINUP GIRL

Won't you be my pinup girl
  And take my breath away.
Won't you wear my gaze,
  Enhance my days with artful play.

Won't you decorate my view
  With everything you are.
Won't you play your part with daring,
  Posture as my star.

Won't you take advantage of me,
  Ravage my resistance.
Won't you let imagination
  Inch away the distance.

Won't you wear those simple things
  That don't amount to much.
Won't you send an invitation
  To the world of touch.

Won't you show me your intent,
  Expose the depth of mine.
Won't you tease and tempt and please
  And let me cross the line.

TAKEN TO EXTREMES

You are my superlative,
  My absolute extreme,
My rising rays of morning,
  My evening's fiery dream.

You cut a racy figure;
  Your pleasure can't be bought;
You wear a world of glamor
  Whenever you wear naught.

You own me without trying;
  You tie my heart up tightly
As I observe with inner passion
  Your disrobing nightly.

You are my only catalyst,
  My sensory Niagara.
You are the lure that pulls me in,
  My virtual Viagra.

Your casual is elegant;
  No makeup mars your look.
You're vibrant and refreshing
  As a tantalizing brook.

So many wrap themselves
  In fancy articles enticing.
Without any wrapping,
  You're my cake and you're my icing.

Passionate Love

THE KISS

Lips meet softly,
    Trading light pressures,
Sharing moist meanings
    In nerve-sweet moments.

Plump pat of love,
    Robbing breath,
Focusing pleasure,
    Warming the senses.

Tender point of contact,
    Stirring passion,
Arousing the heart
    In privileged surprise.

Caress my life fondly
    With private compulsions;
And tempt me to explore
    Your intimate secrets.

LET ME INTO YOUR HEART

I want to bridge the lonely thought
    That you are you and I am I
By letting hopes of "us" and "we"
    Connect our worlds in warm reply.

I want to find a link with love
    So we can both consume its fire.
I want our hearts to be so close
    That we can satisfy desire.

I want the stillness found in peace,
    The joining of two minds.
I want the new discoveries
    Our life together finds.

I want my inner feelings
    To embrace the deeper you.
I want to stretch my vision,
    Bring to love a fuller view.

I want to fit into your dreams,
    Accept a broader part.
So let me into all you are,
    Especially your heart.

A TIME FOR US

In a little space amidst the hurry
    Where the world is free of fuss,
Let's share a moment all our own—
    A special time for us.

Let's shape a quiet interlude,
    Explore our inner being.
Let's see ourselves as only we
    Are capable of seeing.

Let's rediscover hidden moments,
    Times of you and me.
Let's recreate the moods we've known,
    So sensuous and free.

Let's bring our lives together,
    Find the warmth that means so much.
Let's draw our beating hearts so close
    That they can almost touch.

And after hearts have spoken
    And this special time has fled,
A silent closeness, calm and sure,
    Will fill our hearts instead.

YOU TURN ME ON

I'm a captive,
    I'm a pawn
To moments when
    You turn me on.

You stir my senses,
    Fill my mind,
Unleash my passions,
    Make me blind.

You're the strongest
    Of all potions.
You're the key
    To my emotions.

You will it, want it,
    Seek it, take it,
Show it, flaunt it,
    Can't forsake it.

You're an adult;
    You're a child;
You're the one
    Who makes me wild!

I WANT YOU

In a peaceful, perfect moment,
  In a mood of gentle giving,
Let's flow into each other,
  Turn each other on to living.

In a free and open manner,
  In a ritual of senses,
Let's cast off inhibition
  And abandon our defenses.

In a scene of sensuality,
  In the confidence of sharing,
Let's tease and touch and tantalize
  And be a little daring.

In the fullest self-expression,
  In the peace of perfect pleasure,
Let's fuse our hearts together
  And explore love's tender treasure.

YOU ARE JUST A PART OF ME

In after hours' quiet darkness,
　　Letting thoughts unwind,
I fuse with you in form
　　And drink your warmth into my mind.

I draw your spirit closer,
　　Taking in your gentle feeling.
I let our pressures softly blend
　　And fill our hearts with healing.

We're but a single shape,
　　A moving still life of positions.
We fill opposing curves
　　And whisper silent recognitions.

We're unified in touch
　　And feel a wondrous sense of "we."
I pull you in so close
　　That you are just a part of me.

I WANT YOUR LOVE

I want to feel your love for me,
    To sense your warm desire.
I want to know that deep within you
    Embers turn to fire.

I want to see your senses
    Lifted up on passion's wave.
I want to feel your hunger
    For the very things I crave.

I want my heart and mind
    To stir your mind and heart together
And let our tender feelings
    Float the currents like a feather.

I want to touch your body,
    Plot each feature of your form,
Caress the softer details,
    Let emotions gently storm.

I want to merge our movement
    Into one magnetic motion.
I want the fluid force of love
    To build into an ocean.

FAMILIAR GLANCES

Familiar glances lengthened to a stare
    As I absorbed your figure standing there.
The many times you'd stood before my eyes
    Did not reduce the moment's soft surprise.

I felt a little shy to linger so
    But somehow didn't want the time to go.
I knew you wouldn't mind the eyes' caress,
    The touch of vision only I possess.

For me you are no less a work of art,
    Though countless times your view
        Has crossed my heart.
These private moments, purely off the cuff,
    Refresh the soul but never are enough.

With quiet, fleeting thoughts too quick to share,
    My inner feelings penetrate the air;
But sometimes the attraction of your form
    Compels me to reach out and share your warm.

THAT ENERGY CALLED LOVE

That physical focus,
   That river of heart,
That moment of mutual
   Magical art.

The tactile encounter,
   The total surrender,
The feeling of fusion,
   The sipping of splendor.

The tasting and testing,
   The trying and trading,
The helping, assisting,
   Exploring and aiding.

The limitless loving,
   The endless profusion,
The sensuous searching,
   Defying conclusion.

The energy flooding,
   The warmth overflowing,
The passion expanding,
   The dialog growing.

That moment, that minute—
   Obsessive, unending—
When the energy found in two lovers
   Is blending.

STAY CLOSE TO ME

When morning sun is beaming
　　On our silhouetted love
And as I stir I know that
　　You are all I'm thinking of,
　　　　　　Stay close to me.

When birds commence their songs of love
　　And sound their soft alarm
And, lacking inhibition,
　　We are tangled arm in arm,
　　　　　　Stay close to me.

When comfort streams between two bodies
　　Welded side to side
And when there are no secrets
　　For familiar forms to hide,
　　　　　　Stay close to me.

When touching is a tactile treasure
　　We can both explore
And we can sense each other's
　　Inner appetite for more,
　　　　　　Stay close to me.

When love's a true collaboration,
　　Perfect with its flaws,
A joy that needs elaboration,
　　Thriving "just because,"
　　　　　　Stay close to me.

When every mood we share
   Is but an exercise in love
And two unique identities
   Can fit just like a glove,
           Stay close to me.

When we can still experiment,
   Discover something new,
And all the mystery of love
   Is there when I'm with you,
           Stay close to me.

When we can watch the setting sun
   With optimistic eyes
And learn to love the night
   Before the sun begins to rise,
           Stay close to me.

READING FOR PLEASURE

I reach out
        To read your body
            With my hand,
A familiar story
        I return to often,
To soothe my aloneness,
        To bond in ways
            Words can't.

I map your contours,
        Plot your north and south,
            East and west,
Change your chill to warm,
        Knead your ups,
            Read your downs,
Attend your softness,
        Review your hardness.

With healing touch,
        I trace your symmetry,
Reading your reverse,
        Mirroring your opposite
            With fond attention.

I linger across your hill and dale,
    Coddle your in and out,
Discern again each detail,
    Making the known new,
       Relearning every route,
Savoring head to feet,
    Infusing cold with heat,
Researching, rereading, reviewing,
    Blending two
       Into one.

VISUAL POETRY

Your flowing ripe lines of familiar flesh
    Punctuate my vision.
My seasoned eyes return again
    To caress their plenty.

Their fullness frees desire.
    Their roundness perfectly attracts
And tempts my lips
    With their soft gentle sweep.

I train my eyes unselfconsciously
    In loving tribute
To the memories of touch
    So warmly teasing.

My glance drinks in this vintage feeling.
    My arms complete the tactile circuit,
Drawing your near form to my lips,
    To my own press of flesh.

What was imagined now turns real.
    What vision incited loses its clamor.
What memory impressed impresses again.
    What was poetry in motion newly inspires
        And transforms this audience of one.

Love's Universe

OUR UNIVERSE

Alone...
> I looked into the night
> and felt its cold.

Standing together...
> We saw the stars
> and were amazed.

Touching each other...
> We forgot darkness
> and discovered our own universe.

Sharing...
> We explored that universe
> and found it a warmer, better place.

Loving...
> We became aware
> of its infinite depth.

Growing together...
> We wanted our universe
> to endure.

Remaining together...
> We created a beautiful
> synthesis of our dreams.

TIME BEGAN WITH US

Was there a time
    When our fondest emotions
Ran free and untamed
    Like the most distant oceans?

Was there a moment
    In infinite space
When our hearts didn't mesh
    In a loving embrace?

Was there an instant
    In deepest recall
When our spirits and souls
    Weren't together at all?

Was there a past
    Before we had met
When loneliness summoned
    A sense of regret?

Despite all our yesterdays,
    I must confess—
The present is all
    That my heart can possess.

Our loving has conquered
    The past that's within.
When we found each other,
    Time chose to begin.

BEFORE I MET YOU

Before I met you I was just
    A lonely dream in flight,
A heart without an anchor,
    A season without light.

My hopes still craved an answer;
    My spirit sought to grow;
My life still needed someone
    To set my soul aglow.

But when the moment happened
    And we joined in heart and mind,
A life of new discovery
    Was tenderly defined.

We learned to walk the path of sharing—
    Talked and laughed and cared.
Our fondness for each other
    Was in truth and warmth declared.

And soon we knew that passion
    Was the gift that two receive
When they embrace the feeling
    That their love will never leave.

I AM YOURS

The intimate surrender
    My captive heart explores
Permits me to confess
    My deepest feeling—"I am yours."

The loving balance that allows
    Two spirits to combine
Tells my heart to grasp
    The gentle concept, "You are mine."

The limits of our love,
    The widest bounds of our affection,
Attach the fullest meaning to
    Our dreams and our direction.

And when our deep commitment
    Finds a challenge to withstand,
The definition of our love
    Is ready to expand.

"I am yours" is my true pledge,
    Not just a groundless phrase.
My heart is poised with yours
    To plot our love a thousand ways.

FOREVER AND ALWAYS

Forever and always
　　Our love will endure.
Our hopes will grow stronger,
　　Our thoughts more secure.

Forever and always
　　Time will recall
The heat of our passion,
　　The start of it all.

Forever and always,
　　Through darkness and light,
The days will be rich
　　With the promise of night.

Forever and always
　　Our spirits will blend;
Our hearts will join forces,
　　Soft messages send.

Forever and always
　　Our dreams will continue;
And all that I'm looking for
　　I'll find within you.

YOU ARE MY LIFE

Heart by heart
    We hold the truth
        And hear our pulses meeting.
Sense by sense
    We celebrate
        A time that is too fleeting.

Life by life
    We lead each other
        Into dreams of sharing.
Day by day
    We reach into
        The inner core of caring.

Breath by breath
    We blow away
        The loneliness of living.
Self by self
    We move into
        The majesty of giving.

Night by night
    We chase away
        The challenge of the ages.
Heart by heart
    And hope by hope
        We love away life's pages.

FOR MY LOVE

I searched my world for you...
Uncertain of your existence,
I hoped, but sometimes doubted, that I would find you.
I now feel the pressure lifted.
I look and still see those around me;
But my looking and seeing are an affirmation
Of my discovery of you.
As time passes, the gift of chance that you represent
Becomes even more evident and striking.
The improbability of us
As a function of life's chance encounters
Frightens me;
Because if you had not been there when I was,
Or I had not been there when you were,
We wouldn't have found
That miracle of warmth and completeness we now feel.
Were this gift not ours,
Were you not mine,
I would still be searching for you
As a boat in fog seeks its mooring,
As a swimmer his landfall,
As an airborne seed its permanent base of growth.

I LOVE YOU THE MOST

I love you the most
    When we're one thought together,
With purposes joined
    In all shades of weather.

I love you the most
    When our joys and our worries
Engage us with tears of both kinds
    As life hurries.

I love you the most
    When our pace of work pauses
And we can arrange
    A time-out from all causes.

I love you the most
    When we run side by side
Or press in together,
    All secrets confide.

I love you the most
    When we're sassy and show it,
Our hearts murmur passion
    And don't even know it.

I love you the most
    When our spirits are linking,
When we're rich in feelings,
    Not burdened with thinking.

I love you the most
    When we glance at the past
And replay those moments
    That went by too fast.

I love you the most
    When we're partners in time
And every new day
    That we're sharing is prime.

OUR LIFE TOGETHER

Let us spend this life together.
   Let us fill this universe.
Let us call this planet, "Love"—
   A magic place where hearts converse.

Let's define our life of sharing.
   Let us amplify this gift.
Let's be one and two uniquely
   As the seasons float and drift.

Let's grow stronger, never weaken.
   Let's press on and find our dreams.
Let's embrace a precious future—
   See in us the best of teams.

Let us spend this life together
   And in treasured recall hold
Hopes that blossomed, love that flourished,
   Times we tucked away like gold.

Now the sun is rising softly,
   Bathing us in warmth and light.
Love exceeds each new horizon,
   Going far beyond our sight.

VISION OF LOVE

Somewhere in the deep out there
    Another stands alone
Along the narrow bands of time
    Where simple hopes are sown.

Somewhere in the crowded coldness
    Dreams are softly spread
And echo in the isolation,
    Overtaking dread.

Somewhere in the gusts of chance
    A precious time awaits
And holds within unlikely grip
    A challenge to the fates.

Somewhere in an instant
    Two trajectories converge
And from the drifting solitude
    Two sharing hearts emerge.

Somewhere in a body's touch
    And passion's purest voice
A message overtakes the ages,
    Whispering its choice.

Somewhere in a chilling world
    Upon a churning sea
I see a vision of true love
    Embraced in you and me.

WIND WALKING

The scary, majestic
    Aloneness of me
In the crisp
    Early frost of winter
As I mark the moment
    With motion,
        Consume seconds with steps,
Feel the impenetrable
    Depth of time
        Sliding past me.

That frosty exhilaration,
    That crystal cold
As I plunge forward
    With a shiver
        At my shoulder,
            A chill at my neck,
A gentle push of wind
    Squirming into every
        Gap of clothing.

Take me then forward
    Through time,
Along countless beats
    Of heart and motion
To where I am now,
    Crossing days
        Of winter,

With just one adjustment,
    The addition of you,
Slip-streaming me
    Through chill and challenge
And impenetrable depths
    Of time.

Sharing the motion
    Of your step
Reduces the winter
    Of any season
        For a shared time,
            Then for all time,
Until that time, too,
    Reaches a conclusion
Returning once again
    To the scary, majestic
        Aloneness of one,
            Or the other,
                Or, ultimately,
                Neither.

WE SHARE THIS MOMENT

No time but now,
    No day but this,
No place but here—
    Too fine to miss.

The present is
    Our time to share,
Our space to fill,
    Our chance to care.

We press in close,
    We pull in tight,
We grasp the moment,
    Breathe the light.

We find our love,
    We live our dream,
We write our story,
    Launch our theme.

We have a passion
    We explore.
We have the present,
    Nothing more:

No time but now,
    No day but this,
No place but here—
    Too fine to miss.

Love's Timeless Moments

I LOVE YOU MORE EACH DAY

I saw you again today
   For the first time.
Love, you see, has a way of letting us
   Rediscover yesterday's surprises.

Tomorrow, I'll again be alert to you—
   Your words, your appearance,
   Your movement, your touch—
For I'm certain there's something
   I missed today.

Each day I want to discover
   All there is to discover;
But each succeeding day
   My discovery begins anew.

DANCE WITH ME

Dance with me and share my steps
    As we have done before.
Let us merge our forms in warmth
    And drift across the floor.

Flow with me in freedom,
    Let our routine movements vary.
Let's drink the music of the moment,
    Feel our motions marry.

Let's sweep our senses past
    The pounding threshold of our cares.
Let's glide in carefree comfort
    Upon light and buoyant airs.

Let's fuse in feelings physical,
    Escape in cloudless dreams.
Let's slip up to the heavens,
    Swept away on silver beams.

WHEN TIME STANDS STILL

The crystalline perfection
    Of a moment locked in time
Distills its true reflection
    Into memory sublime.

A day when progress halted
    And time, it seemed, stood still,
We sipped of pure simplicity
    And couldn't get our fill.

We focused on the plainer truths;
    We saw with clearer eyes;
We shunned the clutter in our lives
    And thus became more wise.

Life has certain jewels
    That are timeless and are rare.
They captivate us humbly
    In a breath of pure spring air.

A SPACE IN TIME

A crack in true eternal time
    Gives window to existence.
Mortal eyes so poignantly
    Record this precious distance.

Our brief moment lets us love
    This fragile gift of chance,
Filling eyes abundantly
    With life's resplendent glance.

Light my vision with awareness
    Of each fleeting second.
Let my senses shower
    In the warmth of hearts that beckoned.

Let us fill this crack in time
    And occupy our space
In such a way that time will say—
    Now, endlessly embrace.

WE

Time is sifting softly
   Through the moment
      Moving free.
Life is that unlikely
   Stretch of hope
      So briefly we.

Back and forth
   In unison,
      In undulating waves,
We share the test of winds
   That challenge
      All our feeling saves.

Erosively persistent,
   All the hours
      Breathe and blow.
Throughout our modest
   Interlude,
      They tell us we must go.

We ask a little longer,
   Count our seconds
      As we sway,
And hear the winds reply
   That all we offer
      Is today.

IT WAS BEAUTIFUL

Living out life's moments
    We've become caring, sharing
        Passengers
Who voyage through time and space,
    Locked together
        In motion
            And tender dreaming.

The quiet beauty
    And casual eloquence
        Of our lives
Bring harmony and warmth
    And shared hope.

Our spirits are nourished
    In those rest places
        Of the mind
Where time slows just enough
    To still confusion
And sharpen perceptions
    Of the heart.

Such impressions link up
    In a love-inspired continuum
To give us that line of resistance
    Against fear, sadness, regret
And to promote compassion
    And caring.

I look now and again
  At past images
    And future impressions
And think how nice it will be
  If my last mortal image,
    Bountiful and complete,
      Powered by an unending love,
Mirrors the present
  And repeats once again—
    "It was beautiful."

THE PATH WE LEAVE BEHIND

We walked the shores together
  Leaving footprints in the sand.
The cleansing action of the waves
  Behind us licked the land.

We dreamed our way across the sand
  As others had before.
We left our new impressions
  Printed softly on the shore.

And when we turned around
  And later walked again that ground,
We looked for traces left before
  But not a trace was found.

We felt the tidal motion
  Moving up and over feet
And sensed that rare and fleeting
  Gift of chance when spirits meet.

We felt the moist reminder
  That our love's a special place
Where hearts inscribe a message
  For the ages to erase.

And clasping lives we moved ahead
  As nature had designed
And covered all the shores we could
  And never looked behind.

TITLE INDEX

Bruce Wilmer lives and works with his wife, Sydney, in the Blue Ridge Mountains of western North Carolina. They started their own publishing business, Wilmer Graphics, in Huntington, NY in 1976, creating and marketing Bruce's original poetry products worldwide, while raising their two children. They relocated their manufacturing operation to North Carolina in 2003 and launched Winding Brook Press to continue publishing Bruce's poetry books.